From the Cave's jukebox

[Some more Tom Beckett Titles]

Mark Young

Sandy Press

Cover illustration
Tom Beckett pauses at the cave's mouth
by Mark Young

Cover preparation & design
by harry k stammer

ISBN: 979-8-9924582-6-8

Some of these pieces first appeared in:

BlazeVOX, Blood + Honey, dadakuku, Fixator Press, Home Planet
News, Moss Trill, #Ranger, Scud, Synchronized Chaos, The
Saturday Paper, & Utriculi.

My thanks to the respective editors.

Sandy Press
California
https://sandy-press.com/

sandypress@gmail.com

Contents

"All songs listed were written, performed, and recorded
by Vaudeville without Organs."

Tom Beckett; *APPEARANCES; A NOVEL IN FRAGMENTS*,
Moria Press, Chicago, 2015.

n.b. Some of the songs' titles were modified between
their first appearance on Tom Beckett's
l'amour fou blog & their inclusion in his book
APPEARANCES; A NOVEL IN FRAGMENTS.
The original titles have been used here.

Algebraic Bric-a-brac Breakdance

$a^2 + b^2 =$ the unattractive vase — you
know, the one that belonged to grand-
mother & that now sits on a shelf
in what is still grandly described as
the upstairs lounge even though the
hip-hop daughter of the family has
appropriated it for her own purposes
& is even now ensconced there, her

shoulders balancing on the carpet, legs
upright, spinning in a widdershins
direction that brings her feet inexor-
ably closer to the vase which is about to
have its equation solved in a decidedly
unambiguous way. $a^2 + b^2 = (ea^X) + vs^Y)$.

Badiou's Bad IOU Blues

The word as notion. Love is.
Don't the moon look lonesome
shining through the trees? Who
does Badiou owe? Why does he

wish to pay them back? Noun as
an oddment, the minimal form of
communism. 33 words unscram-
bled from the letters in NOTION.

Sent for you yesterday & here you
come today. What is the reason
for his ill will & when did it come
about? Evil is the interruption of

a truth. Can it be comprehended
through listening &/or reading?
How will he achieve his desires?
What use user avatar or wiki user?

Chalk Songlines

The destination decided; & even for those who have never been this way before the directions demonstrated — not by roadmap or satnav but by song. Handed down, learnt. Many generations passed. But who the first? & how determined?

Start with the sky, the passage of the sun, the patterns of the stars. Add on the patterns of the landscape, shaped by the totem of the local nation. Those things known, become the backbone for new journeys. Direction decided by the elders, investigated by the young, who mark their trailblazing with ocher or chalk.

The elders follow those marks, decide what words to use to describe the identifying features, what forms the songs should take to incorporate those words, what songline the traveler should follow to get to where they wish to go.

Data Dump Duet (the remix)

Deduplicate database records. Delete existing migrations. Ancillary data is preserved from the import of MXF files. Write this to tpx1/4c. The Aussie popstar ended up missing the cut.

When writing the mrlithium duet files via cmd, or singing *frozen* with kakulitan medyo mahina data nila dito, the 93c66 immo dump should be put in immobox. I put the ecu

eeprom data into virgin state. Signal K must have been misinterpreting or dumping the sentences in the conversion to SK. What eeprom is in the ecu in systems with AVC-

Intra native recording formats? A printable brain dump duet planner with a green & white color scheme contains a single type-0xEE partition. I'm going out to buy a watermelon.

Erotic Ergonomic Prelude

This one-way nozzle, featured
in an exquisite blue, can be seen

as a prelude to *lock & play*, an ex-
pression that did not appear until the

early 1800s when more widespread,
efficient, & stable manufacturing

processes gained momentum as
an artistic movement in France.

Forgotten Fantasies

"I was saved by doG to make America grate again." — D. J. T.®.

Annie Leibovitz once sought me out to pose for a *Rolling Stone* cover photo wearing only an orange thong.

Barack Obama wanted to come on to *The Apprentice*. He didn't make it past the first screen test. "You're fired!" I told him.

Chelsea Manning was my late night hornpipe-dream until I discovered they weren't the Clinton's daughter.

Donald Jr. upheld his pledge for the family trust to not do deals & investments in foreign countries, as well as not collect payments from foreign governments in its U.S. properties, during my first term in office.

Europe willingly became my fiefdom.

Fans flocked to the T.®umpcon I arranged at the Capitol Building in 2021.

Gerontologists predict that I'm going to live longer than Methuselah.

Haitians lined up in droves to pay homage to me, believing I was the Messiah. I gave visas to those who brought a benison. The remainder begged for beneficence. I don't know what the words mean.

Israelis also believe I'm the Mashiach, the Messiah. I've given them Lebanon & Syria already, & tomorrow when I wake, I'm going to give them Mesopotamia & Persia. I love those old-fashioned names! Next week I'm giving them the Ukraine & China because those countries are going to cost me money & the I.D.F. knows how to handle uppity countries.

Jack Black wanted to falsely indict me for trying to overturn the 2020 election results. I took his Emmy away.

Kelloggs have begun to include T.®ump figurines in their Corn Flakes packets. Anyone who collects twenty of them will be guaranteed a spot in Heaven because, by then, I'll be the centerpiece of the Trinity.

"Let me grab your pussy," I say to every woman I find attractive who I come in contact with & they let me.

Melania doesn't get pissed at me.

"Nearer my God to thee," shout the adoring crowds pressing closer as I pass through them.

Overseas military service is something I would have willingly participated in, but my country needed me elsewhere.

Papa Was a Rollin' Stone was one of the first singles I released. My version made it to No. 1 on the *Billboard* Hot 100.

Queer Theory, as I have often stated, is the philosophy that binds my administration together.

Rand Paul said, in September of 2014, "The President, Barack Obama, acts like he's a king." I've decided to go one step better & proclaim myself one.

Society needs me as an unbiased arbiter. No one else in the world could fill such a role.

Teleprompters are something I do not need. I write my own speeches, remember them, & speak them without notes.

United the States had never been until I came along.

Vladimir Putin has permanently canceled Russia's Victory Parades because he knows they can't compare to mine. Mine's bigger & better in every respect.

Weltherrschaft, world domination, is not something that the Elongated Muskrat & I are deliberately seeking. But should it happen, we both have the ethical & moral fortitude not to take advantage of it.

X has tried to maintain its pace with my Truth Social but can't keep up. It's no contest. See V above.

You only have to see my oversize & illegible & arrogant Sharpied signature on the plethora of executive orders I have executed to know that I'm a man of wealth & taste.

Zelenskyy is a pain in my rectum. When I have a spare afternoon, I'm going to paint him pink, parcel him up, & sell him to the highest bidder.

Ghost Whirl

There aren't many choices in
the context of real music per-
formance now that the bug
category has been changed to
critical & white shapes illumi-
nate the village bakery. Some-
thing went wrong while

submitting the form. Lyrics
for the song have yet to be
transcribed. Nightmare fuel
cells have exploded & set the
transcriber alight in a true pad-
dock-to-plate experience. The
only functioning things left are

rhythms composed of simple
integer ratios, & a mathematical
function that extracts a character
or a specific number of characters
from a text string. As technology
develops, the lines the mind per-
ceives become increasingly faint.

Homophone Nights

Five minutes after I
plug the phrase into
Google, its AI partner
comes awake & tells
me it thinks it's *knights*.
I was on edge there for a
while, worried I may
have keyed in some-
thing that could have
brought the morality
police around. But now
I'm breathing easier, I
return to Google &
enter 'homophobe
knights' which is what
I was going to search
for in the first place
to see if the castle
cloisters were safe for
a struggling minstrel
to stay in overnight.

Haiku Zydeco

Like the chance meeting
of a washboard & a frog
on an airboat — plunk!

Irregular Interventions

Apparently influenced by the concept
of Manifest Destiny, a dominant theme
in the history is a subculture of birds
made queer by endocrine disruptors.

It's a pervasive idea, a form of colon-
ial environmental violence, worked
around an exhaustive dataset of cells
that limit the entry of race into popu-

lations. A supervised machine learn-
ing model to predict pipeline success
in which it is remarkable should a
middle/passive verb occur even twice.

Joint Custody Rhapsody

The two pigeons who caused chaos
aboard a Delta flight had a minor
hit in the early 1990s called "Cow-
boy Lover." A photo of them per-
forming at the 1963 March on
Washington hangs above my bed.

Their aura — that invisible yet vi-
brant energy field which surrounds
all beings — has been a subject of
fascination across centuries &
cultures. But transparent inform-
ation that might help you plan

your dance journey has became
mired in the tangle of biochemis-
try. The factual matrix which
clarifies the pigeons' relationship
to the universe, & your relationship
to both parties, only appears at ir-

regular intervals & promotes a dif-
ferent & always unrelated message
every time. The most recent seen:
"amputation is through the joint."

Karaoke Suicide Stomp

Is there any known footage of Mitch Lucker stomping ...Yes there actually is! It's in the metal footage archives next to ozzy eating a bat and marilyn manson removing his ribs to suck his own dick.

The AI Extrapolation

Google's all-invasive AI Overview beast tells me:

The song "Stomp" by Steps has a karaoke version available, according to Spotify. The title "Karaoke Suicide Stomp" likely refers to the karaoke version of the song "Stomp" and the potential for over-enthusiastic singing in a karaoke setting.

Here's a breakdown:

Karaoke:

A form of entertainment where people sing along to music with lyrics displayed on a screen.

Suicide:

This term is often used humorously in karaoke, referring to the intensity & sometimes questionable vocal choices people make while singing.

Stomp:

The name of a song by the band Steps, which is being used in the context of karaoke.

Therefore, "Karaoke Suicide Stomp" refers to singing the Steps song "Stomp" in a karaoke setting, possibly with a humorous & exaggerated attitude, which is common among karaoke enthusiasts.

Elsewhere

Has been made abundantly clear to those who've had the pleasure of seeing him live, where he totes an aggressive brand of participatory karaoke suicide. It's just great. No other way to spin it.

Elsewhile

The else Statement. With the else statement we can run a block of code once when the condition no longer is true.

Elsewhen

This word is now obsolete. It is last recorded around the late 1500s.

Lactic Acid Rock

It's the berms that did it. Those,
& the mountain bike I'd just
bought. Otherwise, just another
day in paradiddle land. Drum-
set on the handlebars, RLRR the
rhythm pattern that I was after,
too many things on the menu to
comfortably fit into this *l'après-
midi d'un faune* that I'd let my-
self be sucked into. Lactic acid-
osis kicks in, brought about by
the numerous up, over, & down
stressors at the bike/berm inter-
sections. Nor can the height of
the hills be excluded — as that
AC/DC song goes, it's a long way
to the top (if you wanna rock 'n'
roll). As are the coming downs.
Same berms, different rhythm.

Language Gamelan

I quickly get baffled by all the
dialects. Maybe it's those per-
cussive instruments interfering
with my mental processes, even

though there is a belief that the
sound & rhythm can put you
in touch with the universe. The
stars seem so far away. Not so

their music. When I Bluetooth
my cellphone to my earbuds,
some conversations seem to have
a separate sonic accompaniment.

People say it's static. I prefer to re-
gard it in Pythagorean terms, as
music of the spheres, played in a
way that brings Bach back to me.

Multivariate Melodies

Pattern analysis will be employed
to investigate those onset-related
brain responses that occur when
a more abstract dimension of pop-
ular music is introduced. Basal
ganglia — the areas commonly
associated with visceral pain —
are involved which overshadow

the true nature of a key change or
an out-of-key pitch, the usual
markers of an anomaly in any
music acquisition. No longer can
nootropic supplements provide the
mental energy throughout the day
that is needed to complete an audi-
tory scene analysis of polyphony.

Niche Notes

I'm online in Dubai, looking for a
niche-quality fragrance that's right
for special occasions. Not exactly
formal, but giving off a luxurious
impression through its fruity top
notes of, say, violet leaf, peach, or
ylang ylang. But as I dig deeper, I
start to feel as if I'm in the wrong

place. Seems like niche apparently
does not necessarily mean attract-
ive to the olfactory organs. I read:
*the best niche fragrances for beginners
are art forms.*[1] I read: *Still life with
grape soda, rotting fruits, & oysters.*[2]
I read: *notorious for being "the
most disgusting scent in the world."*[2]

[1] *Besuited Aroma*, 12/21/2022
[2] *Fragrantica*, 6/4/2024

Open Letter Operetta

Librettist:

You don't need a
letter opener to
open a letter when
it's an open letter.

Director:

That's great! Now if we repeat that a number of times then that's the operetta
half-written already. What characters did you have in mind?

Librettist:

Was thinking of a cheated-on partner as lead, a mezzo-soprano, a bit of a
Taylor Swift voice. Other characters would include the non-singing postal
worker who brought a letter from the partner in which they admit their
cheating & end with an unapologetic goodbye. The contents of the letter
could be sung by the departing partner from a position near the back of the
stage.

To go with that, perhaps partly performed as a contrapuntal overlap with the
preceding:

Today the post-
woman brought
me a letter from my
ex-partner. I will

not open it be-
cause I am al-
ready aware of
what it will say.

To follow on, we have a scene where the spurned spouse sings or speaks their
response as they post it to Facebook or another platform since something that
appears on social media can be framed as an open letter for contemporary
times.

We must, however, in order to adhere to the spirit of an operetta, retain some comedic aspects even though this is essentially a sad piece. Perhaps introduce a chorus who individually comment on the response, &, collectively, interrupt with a repetitive response such as "letter opener, open letter" or "never getting back together again."

Postmodern Polka

At first glance oxymoronic, yet there is an overlap.

Both parts autobiographical. The teenaged bassist, classically trained but now playing pizzicato, filling in at the local Polish Association's New Year's Ball — 57 varieties of potato salad, & just as many polkas — wearing an occasion-obligatory tuxedo borrowed from his father, one pants leg folded up a little bit because his father was lame, had one leg shorter than the other. That was one uncomfortable memory; another that the other three members of the quartet each received twice as much as this fill-in bassist, a fact revealed inadvertently when the organizer asked the band to play for a longer time, &, in offering an additional inducement, admitted what he had already paid.

The postmodern part comes a few years later, when the musician, now tired of carrying his bass around balanced on his shoulder because most taxis in the city were too compact to contain it, discovered he had a small ability with words.

Quadratic Cha-cha

A variable is raised to the power of two (squared).

hip rotate half circle to right

This operation is denoted by a superscript "2" after the variable.

transfer weight to left foot

In medieval manuscripts, many superscript signs were used to abbreviate text.

hip rotate half circle to right

Abbreviations are often divided into three types: suspensions, contractions, & symbols.

hip rotate half circle to left

Typographically, the ampersand, representing the word et, is a space-saving ligature of the letters e & t, its component graphemes.

left foot to side, chasse right

The symbol was so popular in the early 1800s it was added to the end of the English alphabet as the 27th letter .

very small step

It sounded strange to say and and, so people said "x, y, z, and *per se* and," because *per se* meant "by itself."

lateral movement (minimal rotation)

"Killing two birds with one stone" would probably make sense if you said it to someone in context.

hip does continuous figure 8 even on chasse for movement.

Reel for the Real

Cast a line & run what you
reel in through a thesaurus
just to see how real it is.

Remember to allow some
variation for the water you
caught them in. Flat earth

will be different to teenage
turbulence, as will MAGA's
misleading polemics com-

pared with magma cast up
from the bowels of the sea
no matter how much the

former is trumped up & X-
altered.

Sonic Shadows

An anthropomorphic black hedge-
hog with high specificity & sensitivity
explodes on stage declaiming "a posi-
tive is positive!" Really? So sure of

themselves? But then, I guess that's
what specificity means in a testing
environment. Another hedgehog e-
merges from the shadows, smiles at

the audience &, in a confidential tone,
says to them "I'm not that sensitive,
but all this talk of testing makes my
testes hurt. Oh boy, am I blue today."

The Tingle Tango

Written for beginner string groups
in a classy yet sassy style, it provides

the perfect heat for all your dishes &
can also be used as a tanning accele-

rator. From start to finish it provides
unbiased political news &, for a few

dollars more, informed racing inform-
ation so that you can take advantage

of Jonbon being all class & certain to
retain the annual Tingle Tangle title.

Unheimlich Maneuvers

Das Herz ist nicht dort, wo das Heim ist.
— Johann Goiter

The absent-member maneuver is viewed as protecting a psychopathological dyadic alliance &, indirectly, other dyads representing pre-oedipal psychic defenses in schizophrenic families.

The BBQ Roll Maneuver is a therapeutic exercise designed to relieve symptoms of horizontal canalithiasis by repositioning dislodged otoconia within the inner ear.

The Credé maneuver is a technique used to void urine from the bladder of an individual who, due to disease, cannot do so without aid.

The Dix-Hallpike maneuver is a test that healthcare providers use to diagnose benign paroxysmal positional vertigo (BPPV) — a common type of vertigo.

The Epley maneuver or repositioning maneuver is a maneuver used by medical professionals to treat BPPV of the posterior or anterior canals of the ear.

Freiberg's maneuver of forceful internal rotation of the extended thigh elicits buttock pain by stretching the piriformis muscle.

The purpose of the Gufoni maneuver is to reposition any dislodged otoconia from the semicircular canals back to the utricle, where they no longer cause symptoms of dizziness or vertigo.

The homo sapiens maneuver consists of pretending any person you are forced to spend time with is an intelligent human being & not the asshole fuckwit they really are.

The Inspiration maneuver decreases intrathoracic pressure, which simultaneously increases venous flow into the right ventricle (RV) & decreases pulmonary venous flow into the left heart.

The jaw-thrust maneuver is a noninvasive, manual means to help restore upper airway patency when the tongue occludes the glottis, which commonly occurs in patients who are obtunded or unconscious.

The Kocher manoeuvre is a surgical procedure to expose structures in the retroperitoneum behind the duodenum & pancreas.

The Leopold maneuver is a systematic method of abdominal palpation used to assess fetal position, presentation, & engagement in the third trimester of pregnancy.

The McRoberts maneuver is a procedure to correct shoulder dystocia during childbirth. Shoulder dystocia is when the baby's shoulders are stuck inside the pelvis during delivery. It's performed by pressing a pregnant woman's legs against her abdomen.

The necrophiliac maneuver is persuading oneself that the act is not just a defilement before the gods, as much as something that occurs in the natural order of things.

The Oriental maneuver is not a recognized term. However, the 3rd Maneuver Platoon of 1st Davao Occidental Provincial Mobile Force Company serves multiple important purposes, including Campaign Against Loose Firearms & Combating Motorcycle Riding in Tandem Criminals.

In a Palpatation mameuver, press laterally on the edge of a bulla or on suspected necrotic epidermis in Stevens-Johnson syndrome/toxic epidermal necrolysis (SJS/TEN) or pemphigus vulgaris.

The Quasimodo maneuver is performed on a surfboard, where the surfer is riding a wave & extends his arms out parallel to the surfboard & ducks his head.

In the Ritgen maneuver the fetal chin is reached for between the anus & coccyx & pulled interiorly, while using the fingers of the other hand on the fetal occiput to control speed of delivery.

The squatting maneuver simultaneously increases venous return to the right heart & increases afterload & peripheral resistance.

The Toynbee maneuver takes a different approach to opening your eustachian tubes. Rather than forcing air into them, this way helps to open the tubes. That allows air to get in.

An Undulating Maneuver is a soulbind trait granted by Plague Deviser Marileth. When struck by a snare, you drop a puddle that lasts for 10 sec. Enemies that step in the puddle are slowed by 70% for 5 sec. It is exclusive with [Viscous Trail].

The Valsalva maneuver involves forceful exhalation against a closed glottis, straining as if trying to have a bowel movement, initially developed to expel fluids & foreign bodies from the middle ear.

The Wood Screw maneuver is commonly used in orthopedics, particularly in the reduction of dislocated joints. By applying rotational force, the maneuver realigns the joint components, facilitating proper healing.

The xylophone maneuver is a procedure whereby beating on a patient's head with mallets will eventually drive the demons away.

The Yacovino maneuver, also known as the Deep Head Hanging maneuver, is a therapeutic technique developed to manage a rare subtype of BPPV.

The Zavanelli maneuver is an emergency obstetric procedure that involves pushing the fetus's head back into the uterus & then delivering the baby via an emergency cesarean section.

Virtual Memories

Motorcycle wokeness did not
manifest itself until after
Mother had died. At least that's
how I remember it. I woke up,
was told Mother had passed,
went out & bought myself a

two wheel beast. Not a Harley —
Mother would never forgive me
for doing that — but rather one
of those 750cc Japanese models
that you ride sedately on only
if that's what you want to do.

Will overtake most anything that
you'll find on the highway apart
from the odd kangaroo. Which
is what happened to me; & now
I'm in a coma, have no conscious
memories, am virtually a corpse.

Waking Windows

Judging by the size of the
promotional photos, Palehound
& Cut Worms are the headline
acts at this year's final WW music,
art, comedy, food, & drink festival
in Winooski, Vermont. Elsewhere
someone asks: "What is a paw-
paw?" while they're enjoying
drag queen hour which includes
getting their face painted. & over-
seas, at the European Parliament,
#TheLightsStayOn, a photo ex-
hibition presenting powerful
stories of people from Ukraine,
draws inspiration from René
Magritte's *L'état de veille* (*The
Waking State*), where glowing
windows appear in the sky
among drifting clouds. So, to
stop Windows waking up from
sleep on its own, the last band
will wrap up around 10 p.m.

XXL Largo

Now that the wet season
has arrived, I go surfing
before I go surfing, hoping
to find some johnnie O
swim shorts in an extra
extra large size which also
have some length to them.

eBay offers me a pair for $89,
described as having a Conch
Floral design, lined, & with
a drawstring. The Adidas
equivalent at Amazon also
has a drawstring, is in a Rip-
stop 100% recycled polyester

but is currently out of stock.
In the same breath — or at
least on the same page — Ali-
baba.com, under the sub-cat-
gories of Sex Toys / Dildos,
has a Ready to Ship Big XXL
Largo Penis Enlargement

Cream with a 2-year shelf
life. Sterilization, cleaning, &
a free sample are included. They
say they support private labels
& can manufacture to a custom-
er's own design (OEM) or relabel
Alibaba products (ODM). It

also is currently unavailable.
Still surfing, I find I can buy a
Ralph Lauren Polo sweater —
Talle XXL, Largo 80cm, Ancho
70cm — for a mere $33,000; or,
at the other end of the scale, an

XXL long custom "stromboli"

mousepad with a list price of
€44.00. If that was what the
sweater cost I might be inter-
ested; but most everything I've
seen so far seems to have little
to do with surfing, or is out of
stock, or is way too expensive.

Time to stop; so a last entering
of the search term. I goof, leave
off the size's L, so, when I enter,
Chopin & YouTube are every-
where. 24 Preludes, Op. 28: XX.
No. 20 in C Minor (Largo). It's a
nice piece, so I sit back & enjoy.

Yo Yo Mass

I hear noises coming out
of the attic. I go upstairs
to find a Catholic priest
bouncing up & down on
a trampoline. Except there
is no trampoline. Instead,
a raised platform on which
stands a Cardinal manipu-
lating a pair of resistance
bands which pass under the
priest's arms to bounce him
up & down. *Dominus vo-*
biscum says the Cardinal.
Et cum spiritu tuo responds
the priest on the upswing.
Sursum corda adds the man
almost hidden in a corner
of the attic. *Tibi canerem*
he continues, *nisi quod*
violoncellum meum in cista
raedae reliqui, domum
revertens post recentem con-
centum in Aula Carnegie.

Zombified Zydeco

Gris-gris will not help
if you're considered woke
& in danger of being can-
celed. That, thanks to the
current prevalence of far-
right & MAGA views in
Louisiana, presents as a
modern version of being
turned into a zombie. So,
too, cultural things — po-
boy sandwiches, zydeco.

An introduction; though when finished will be an afterword.

During my trawling through past posts & pages for *100 Titles From Tom Beckett*, I rediscovered a January 2013 entry on Tom's *l'amour fou* blog. He posted:

> Anyway, in a section of Appearances that I'm working on now I list titles of imaginary songs that appear on an imaginary jukebox in an imaginary bar called the Cave, a very special club house for the legendary performance art group Vaudeville without Organs.
>
> A jukebox is a treasure trove of information about the sort of establishment it exists within. Herewith a list, alphabetically sorted, of a few of the song titles in the Cave's jukebox . . .

followed by a list of a list of sixteen titles, & a closing message:

> Mark, you're welcome to any of these titles if you're looking for some.

I can't claim not to have seen this post since, in the comments box, is the following:

> (from) mark young January 2, 2013 at 2:52 AM
> You been a peepin at my wurlitzer again!

Jukeboxes are a shared pleasure. On my side, I've lost track of how many times — posts & poems — I've referred to those songs that rise unbidden to the surface of what I call my juxebox of the mind. In what is admittedly a very belated response, I've begun pushing the buttons on this refound Wurlitzer to see what wonders we can wring from it.

Starting tomorrow, the first poem in the series. The remainder will follow at irregular intervals.

gamma ways, September 2, 2024